THIS IS THE HOUSE GEORGE BUILT!

A KID'S GUIDE TO MOUNT VERNON

Bellissima Publishing, LLC
Jamul, California
www.bellissimapublishing.com

ISBN 1-935118-83-8
First Edition

Dedication

To George and Martha Washington and to all the presidents
and first ladies who came after them

And to the Mount Vernon Ladies' Association
who keep Mount vernon open 365 days a year

Introduction

Mount Vernon was the home of the first President of the United States, George Washington. It is located on the banks of (and looks down upon) the Potomac River. Mount Vernon was declared a National Historic Landmark in 1960 and is listed in the National Register of Historic Places.

When Augustine Washington owned the estate, it was known as Little Hunting Creek Plantation. Lawrence Washington, George's older half-brother, inherited the estate and changed the name to Mount Vernon in honor of the Vice Admiral Edward Vernon, Lawrence's commanding officer in the British Navy. When George Washington inherited Mount Vernon he kept the name. But the M ount Vernon is hardly the same property he inherited, from his brother, because he expanded the house and made it his own. This is why it is truly the house that George built!

Once again Penelope Dyan and John D. Weigand have combined efforts to create a book for kids that is fun and educational and looks great on your coffee table. Dyan has taken her talents as a former teacher and put them to work in her own very special way. The photography of John D. Weigand hits the mark again with his unqiue available light only photographs.

This Is The House George Built!

Bellissima Publishing, LLC

This Is The House George Built!

A Kid's Guide To Mount Vernon

Photography By John D. Weigand
Poetry by Penelope Dyan

George Washington inherited a house on a hill,
He rebuilt it and expanded it and it stands there still.
By the name Mount Vernon we know this house best,
Because it is a very famous and old address.
Washington inherited it from his older half-brother.
When he finished building on to it, it was like no other.
He married Martha and built her a wing,
Providing for family was George Washington's thing,
And even though Queen Elisabeth II considered it small.
For their needs they had it all.

They had a barn, a given of course;
They had lots of animals and more than one horse.
They had chickens, cattle, cows and sheep,
That all contributed in some way to their keep.

To the main house the clerk's quarters were near,
Because Washington had lots of paperwork, I fear.
It was only one room, but the clerk had no wife,
And taking care of George's papers was a part of his life.

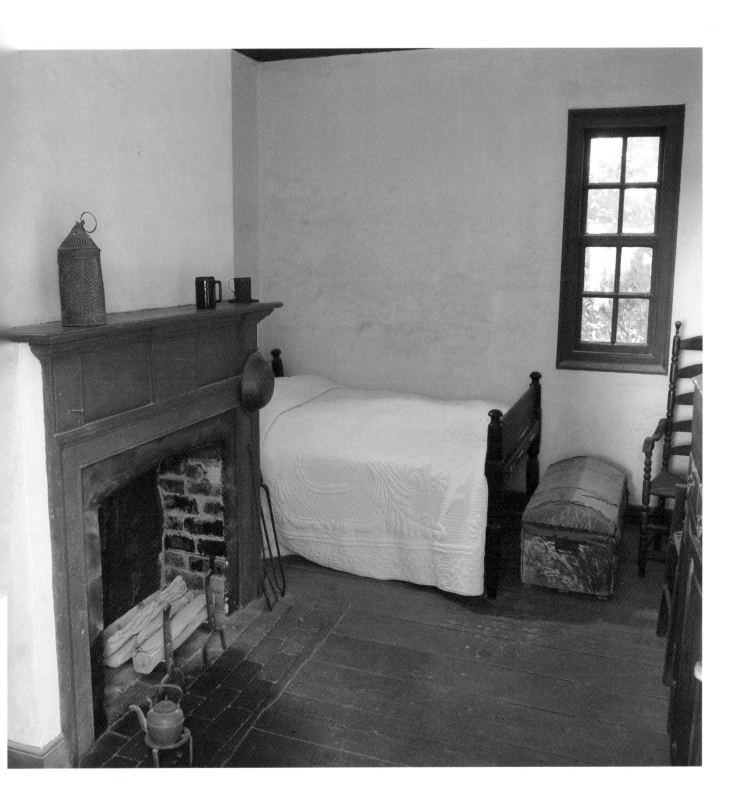

This was once a hospital on these grounds,
(And even though the doctor still made his rounds)
George made this building the gardener's house,
Upstairs and downstairs. . .did you see a mouse?

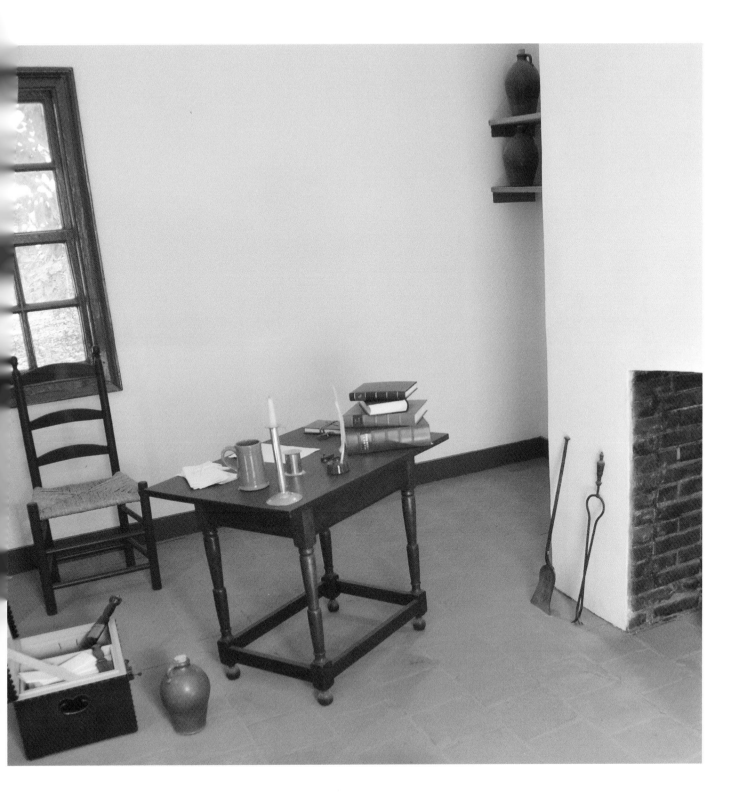

This is the greenhouse I am told,
A place to grow plants when the weather turned cold.

The overseer lived here and when Washington traveled,
He made quite certain the place never unraveled.

There are slaves quarters with table, chairs, fireplace and beds
Where Washington's slaves lay down their heads.
And I am sorry, and it is sad to say,
That many people had slaves in George Washington's day.

The blacksmith took care of horse shoes, utensils and pots,
And as to that work, it seemed he had lots!

A paint cellar stored paint brushes and stuff,
So as of these things there would be enough.

The smokehouse smoked all the meat,
To preserve everything tender and sweet.

And the Spinning house held spinning wheels. . .

And looms where clothes and other things were made,
And as to all the necessities, Mt. Vernon met the grade.

The wash house for washing made things clean and bright.
This was for the Father of Our Country, and this was only right.

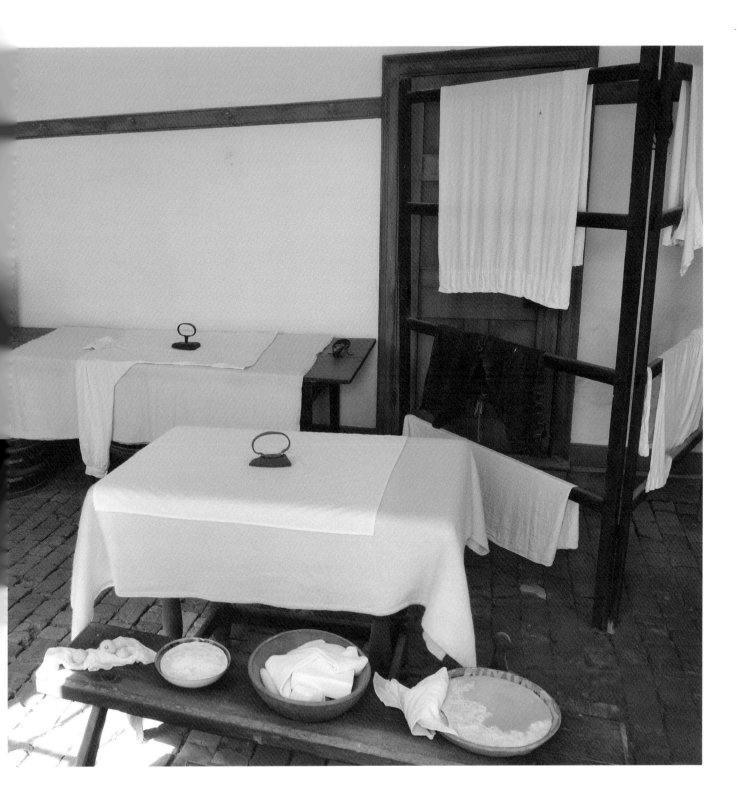

There was a shoemaker's house where shoes were cut and sewn,
And everyone there had shoes made that were their own.
And another thing happened there.
The shoes were kept in good repair.

George washington had a riding chair, in the style of the day.
He used the chair quite often as he went out upon his way.
It didn't move all by itself, of course,
As it was pulled by a fine steed of a horse.

And here we have George Washington's carriage,
(He probably used it for his marriage.)
Because he had to get to the church on time,
And his bright red carriage was VERY fine.

Here we see dressed from his head to his toes,
George's Washington's doctor as everyone knows.
And even though we know he's an actor playing a part,
We did see him as we left and from him did depart.
He was quite cordial and very knowledgeable too,
And he will impart his great knowledge you.
He will relate Mount Vernon's story,
As it stood then and stands now in its glory.
And you will say after all is said and done,
That visiting Mt. Vernon was most certainly fun!

The End
"of the sheep's tail"